BLESSINGS ABOUND
Awaken to the Gifts at Hand

Katherine Scherer
Eileen Bodoh

Copyright 2025 Katherine Scherer and Eileen Bodoh of Milwaukee, WI. All rights reserved. No part of this publication may be reproduced, stored in a retrieval system, or transmitted, in any form or by any means, electronic, mechanical, photocopying, recorded, or otherwise, without the proper written permission of the authors.

Cover design by Shelby Keefe, Artist, of Milwaukee, WI

Richard A. Bowen, Editor, of Brookfield, WI

Disclaimer: The authors do not intend this book to encourage any specific religion or teaching, but only to show how blessed we all are.

Disclaimer: The authors did not use AI-Generated content.

Published by K & E Innovations LLP
6099 Oakwood Lane, W
Greendale, WI 53129
Phone: 414-347-1165 or 414-367-2356

Contact Information

Katherine Scherer: chattykathy811@aol.com
Eileen Bodoh: eileenbodoh@charter.net

ISBN: 9780974855011

Contents

PROLOGUE i

A PERSONAL JOURNEY 1

LIFE IS A MYSTERY 1

THOUGHTS TO PONDER 2

YOUR DESTINY... 2

BLESSINGS RECEIVED 5

    LOVE 6

    INNATE BLESSINGS 8

    FREE WILL 10

    HAPPINESS 12

BLESSINGS TAKEN FOR GRANTED 15

    HEART 16

    NATURE 19

    THE BLESSINGS OF MUSIC 24

    THE BLESSINGS OF BEAUTY 27

    A Sleeping Mystery 27

BLESSINGS FOUND IN DISGUISE 30

    THE POWER OF BLESSINGS 31

    BLESSED FRIENDSHIPS AND RELATIONSHIPS 35

    WE ARE HERE FOR EACH OTHER 37

    BLESSINGS OF OLD 39

A WORD ABOUT GOD	42
SPIRITUAL BLESSINGS	42
THE BEATITUDES	43
ONLY GOD	44
EPILOGUE	45

*"Whatever hour God has blessed you with,
take it with a grateful hand."*
–Horace

PROLOGUE

This is a book that reveals how truly blessed you are. In it you will find three categories:

1. ***Blessings Received*** *point to the spirit of life and how it prevails.*

2. ***Blessings Taken For Granted*** *point to unrealized treasures.*

3. ***Blessings Found In Disguise*** *point to a river of peace, harmony, and joy.*

In the midst of daily challenges, you will gain a new perspective to live and work from a place of peace, awe, and wonder.

Recognizing blessings helps eliminate complaining, live from a more positive attitude, and realize temporary failures are nothing more than blessings in disguise. Blessings shower us with good will and love for strength, hope, healing and happiness.

"Blessing, rightly understood, is the invisible bloodstream pulsating through the universe-alive and life-giving." –Brother David Steindl-Rast, www.gratefulness.org (quoted with permission)

Blessings are an enlightening presence in every one's life. Those who allow them into their awareness find them meaningful in their own life, and in the lives of family and friends too. They count their blessings every day, and so can you.

"What is a blessing? A blessing is a circle of light drawn around a person to protect, heal and strengthen..."–John O'Donohue, To Bless the Space Between Us: A Book of Blessings

A PERSONAL JOURNEY

Have you recognized life as your own personal journey? If you have, good; if not, get ready for some eye-opening treasures.

You come into this world by yourself and you leave this world by yourself, but you are never alone. During your time here you will encounter countless thoughts of wonder as to who you are, why you are here, and what to expect.

"...The universe is transformation: life is opinion."
–Marcus Aurelius, Meditations, IV, 3.

LIFE IS A MYSTERY

Born into this world in innocence, life is a gift freely given to you. You are blessed from your very beginning. Your growth from baby to childhood to teenager and then adult are all miracles in process mostly taken for granted. How you grow, how fast you learn, how much you strive and hope for are all blessings freely given to you.

THOUGHTS TO PONDER

Man has control over nothing except the use of his own thought.

"Your beliefs become your thoughts,
Your thoughts become your words,
Your words become your actions,
Your actions become your habits,
Your habits become your values,
Your values become your destiny."
–Mahatma Gandhi

"To believe in the things you can see and touch is no belief at all–but to believe in the unseen is a triumph and a blessing." –Abraham Lincoln

YOUR DESTINY

Mankind has forever wondered if his destiny is his own to choose or if it has already been chosen for him. Sometimes it seems that you have had no choice in the matter. However, when you consider the power in your thoughts you might determine that you had more choice than you ever imagined.

"Most of the shadows of this life are caused by standing in one's own sunshine." –Ralph Waldo Emerson

Positive versus Negative

Your outer world is a reflection of your inner world. Listening to your inner thoughts will help you determine if your thoughts are mostly positive or mostly negative.

Why is this important to know?

When your thoughts are more positive than negative, you will attract more positive things into your life.

What is even *more* important to know is this:

Shifting your thoughts from negative to positive is as easy as <u>counting your blessings</u>.

Did you know that you can only think one thought at a time?

Thinking a negative thought over and over again and expecting a positive result is said to be the definition of insanity.

It is utterly impossible to bless and be in judgment at the same time. Seeing the blessings in your own life attracts more love, more beauty, and more opportunity to you every day.

"All the flowers of all the tomorrows are in the seeds of today." –Indian Proverb

BLESSINGS RECEIVED

The spirit of life prevails

LOVE

Human or Divine?

Whether it is a parent's love for their child, undying love for friends and family, or passionate love for a life partner, none seems as great a love when given to another when nothing is asked in return.

"The love we give away is the only love we keep."
–Elbert Hubbard

Divine love gives blessings with no expectation in return and is the epitome of true love that one can only hope to emulate over time.

Human love clings to selfish love while divine love is unconditional.

"Love is the bridge between you and everything."
–Rumi

No doubt we definitely feel blessed when we feel love. Love sows the seeds of goodwill and reaps the harvest of joy and peace.

"Love does not dominate; it cultivates." –Johann Wolfgang von Goethe

There is a spiritual realm in your life, and it comes to you through divine love.

"Even after all this time the sun never says to the earth, 'You owe me.' Look what happens with a love like that, it lights the whole sky." –Hafiz

INNATE BLESSINGS

Innate - Inborn - Natural

Innate blessings are a quality or tendency present in an individual from birth. Besides taste, touch, smell, sight, and hearing there are many blessings we think little about or take for granted. Hearts beat without direction, breathing air in and out flows easily. Solutions come to our challenges without much thinking.

"Life holds so many simple blessings, each day bringing its own individual wonder." –John McLeod

The names of people with extreme ingrained traits and talents boggle most minds. Musically talented Beethoven and Mozart along with Leonardo da Vinci and his artistic ability are just a few forever remembered.

"What a piece of work is a man!..." –William Shakespeare

Granted, most of us do not have these extreme qualities, yet we must not forget to honor the traits we have. Our sense of justice keeps many on the straight and narrow while those with a fun sense of humor may limit our sense of seriousness. Curiosity leads to positive development that serves mankind, and good organizational skills bring direction to chaos. Innate qualities are blessings indeed.

"And that all the things of the universe are perfect miracles, each as profound as any." –Walt Whitman

FREE WILL

The Gift of Choice

Free will is an innate blessing. **Possibly, it is the greatest of all blessings.** Free will allows full control of your choices and actions. It's a unique tool to indulge in noble or ignoble pursuits resulting in happiness, sadness, joy, or heartache. Never underestimate the gift of free will. It is truly a blessing bestowed upon you.

"The winds of grace blow all the time. All we need to do is set our sails." –Sri Ramakrishna Paramahamsa

Free will shapes your life. Whether choosing goodness or doing whatever you please, there are consequences to your choices. The choices you make determine your success or failure.

"…But with every deed you are sowing a seed, Though the harvest you may not see…." –Ella Wheeler Wilcox

Marcus Aurelius in his words of wisdom said:

"You have power over your mind-not outside events. Realize this, and you will find strength." – Meditations

HAPPINESS

An Inside Job

Are you happy? Or are you like so many people waiting for someone or something else to come along and make you happy? Finding the perfect partner, a higher paying job, or simply a job you love may be some of the things you think will make you happy. And they will - for awhile. But that happiness is short lived and here's why:

"Happiness is a condition of mind not a result of circumstances." –John Lubbock

People and things do not have the power to make us happy. Happiness is an inside job and each of us is responsible for our own happiness.

Mahatma Gandhi defines happiness this way:

"Happiness is when what you think, what you say, and what you do are in harmony."

And Henry David Thoreau says this:

"Happiness is like a butterfly; the more you chase it, the more it will elude you, but if you turn your attention to other things, it will come and sit softly on your shoulder."

A rich full life is filled with joy and sorrow, for it is true we cannot have one without the other. Those who are happy love to create, want to serve others, and are thankful for their blessings. Their own happiness grows as they bring joy to others.

"The unthankful heart...discovers no mercies; but let the thankful heart sweep through the day and, as the magnet finds the iron, so it will find, in every hour, some heavenly blessings!" –Henry Ward Beecher

Shutting our hearts and minds to our dreams can stop our expectations of happiness. Allowing yourself to experience every bit of joy life has to offer increases your capacity for happiness. Happiness is an immeasurable blessing.

"To multiply your joy, count your blessings."
–J. B. Priestley

Today, I am thankful for:

The joy I give,
The laughter I share,
The humor I smile,
The happiness within me.

And remember what Abraham Lincoln said:

"Folks are usually about as happy as they make their minds up to be."

BLESSINGS TAKEN FOR GRANTED

Treasures unknown to you

HEART

Listen to the voice in your heart...

Can you hear it?

Does it fill your spirit?

Is it filled with wisdom from your soul?

The heart is a beautiful thing. Besides pumping two gallons of blood every minute, amazingly it pumps without interruption every day for sixty, seventy, and even eighty years or more.

The Heartmath Solution written by Doc Childre and Howard Martin, with Donna Beech, provides new evidence of the power of heart intelligence. Their book tells of an exciting discovery that the heart has an independent nervous system referred to as "the brain in the heart."

My head said yes, but my heart said no.

The heart is sensitive to every emotion, and all positive or negative energy affects it instantly. It sends intuitive signals to help govern your life.

Independently the heart starts beating in the unborn fetus before the brain has been formed. Wanting to bring a kinder heart into your life is a positive thing.

"A good heart 'is worth gold." –William Shakespeare

When your core heart feelings include love, appreciation, good judgment and care, others will be attracted to you simply because of your transformational heart energy.

Knowing your heart can be beneficial, it's how you relate to life. If you are rigid and keep your heart guarded, the flow of love for others will be shut off and relationships will suffer.

"A loving heart is the truest wisdom." –Charles Dickens

There is no doubt the heart plays an important role in your overall well-being. Love and positive feelings are somehow related to sound health in this stressful world.

"The ripples of the kind heart are the highest blessings of the Universe." –Amit Ray

Which is most important, the head or the heart?

Some say the heart is the most important, while others say it is the brain. The power in your mind can direct you to think good thoughts. The power of the heart is to live from thoughts of love which create the source of life's energy.

"Blessed are the hearts that can bend; they shall never be broken." –Albert Camus

Tapping into the love and happiness of living is not as difficult as you might think. Love and happiness lie in the heart as well as compassion and forgiveness being its treasures. Use your heart as well as your head to determine what is best for you.

"For as he thinketh in his heart, so is he."
–Proverbs 23:7

Blessings abound when your heart is perceived as "the organ of love."

"I looked in temples, churches, and mosques. But I found the Divine within my heart." –Rumi

NATURE

God's handwriting is evident in every nook and cranny.

When we commune with nature, blessings appear all around us enriching our souls. All we have to do is stop, look, and listen.

"...Whether we look, or whether we listen, We hear life murmur, or see it glisten;..." –James Russell Lowell, *"June" from 'The Vision of Sir Launfal'*

Aristotle said:

"In all things of nature there is something of the marvelous."

Dew drops twinkle in the morning silence.

"Every blade of grass has its Angel that bends over it and whispers, 'Grow, grow.'" –The Talmud

A crocus peeps out through melting snow.

"A flower blossoms for its own joy." –Oscar Wilde

Perennial flowers return year after year.

"...And then my heart with pleasure fills, And dances with the daffodils." –William Wordsworth, "The Daffodils"

Puffy, white clouds drift across a deep blue sky.

"Beautiful cloud! with folds so soft and fair, Swimming in the pure quiet air!..." –William Cullen Bryant "To a Cloud"

Glorious rays of sunshine filter through a lifting fog.

"A cloudy day is no match for a sunny disposition."
–William Arthur Ward

A multicolored rainbow appears during a summer shower.

"My heart leaps up when I behold
A rainbow in the sky:..." –William Wordsworth "My Heart Leaps Up"

Flowers in the garden wave to passersby.

"The earth laughs in flowers." –Ralph Waldo Emerson

A sweet-smelling flower is kissed by a honey bee.

"Bees sip honey from flowers and hum their thanks when they leave...." –Rabindranath Tagore

One season flows into the next.

"Nature gives to every time and season some beauties of its own;..." –Charles Dickens

Daylight follows the night.

"...When night comes, the flower folds its petals and slumbers with Love, and at dawn, it opens its lips to receive the Sun's kisses..." –Kahlil Gibran, Tears and Laughter

Grandiose waters tumble down a mountainside.

"...Nature sings her exquisite song...." –James McNeill Whistler

Baby pine trees grow up for Santa.

"Pass then through this little space of time...and end thy journey in content, just as an olive falls off when it is ripe, blessing nature who produced it, and thanking the tree on which it grew." –Marcus Aurelius, Meditations, IV, 48

A morning walk in the park inspires self-talk of how at one we are with nature.

"Hello my little dearest,
My precious little star,
How a mind so purest,
And a heart never far.
In the morning sunlight you glisten as you walk,
While all the trees and flowers bow over with gossip
talk.
How radiant are your teardrops,
Your smiles and kisses too,
Everything in nature was made to honor you."
–Eileen Bodoh

"...Hear blessings dropping their blossoms around you..."–Rumi

"In music, in the sea, in a flower, in a leaf, in an act of kindness...I see what people call God in all these things." –Pablo Casals

THE BLESSINGS OF MUSIC

An Incredible Gift

Captivating hearts and minds with its enchanting melodies and rhythms, music is an integral part of humanity. It shapes cultures and societies around the world. Its transformative power connects us with others.

"Music washes away from the soul the dust of everyday life." –Berthold Auerbach

- It lifts our moods;
- Can be used as a healing tool;
- Eases our pain and anxiety;
- Boosts our productivity;
- Consoles us when we are sad;
- Moves us to recall memories;
- And helps us express our emotions.

Henry Wadsworth Longfellow famously said:

"Music is the universal language of mankind."

Composers have written much in their music about blessings. In the song, "May the Good Lord Bless and Keep You," (written by Meredith Wilson and recorded by countless artists over the years) a wish that our troubles be small, that we walk with sunlight and experience silver linings on every cloud, are words that tug at our heartstrings.

Louis Armstrong's trademark song "What a Wonderful World" tells of the bright blessed day, the colors of the rainbow, skies of blue and pretty faces walking by. What a wonderful world we are blessed with!

Irving Berlin reminds us to count our blessings instead of sheep when we're worried and cannot sleep.

And Karen Drucker's chant "I Am So Blessed" reminds us with simple words to be grateful for our blessings:

> *"I am so blessed*
> *I am so grateful for all that I have*
> *I am so blessed*
> *I am so blessed*
> *I am so grateful*
> *I am so blessed."*

–Works and music Karen Drucker
www.karendrucker.com (quoted with permission)

"Music is the language of the spirit. It opens the secret of life bringing peace, abolishing strife." –Kahlil Gibran

Music can be found and heard everywhere.

- National anthems are played at sporting events;
- Carols fill the air at Christmas time;
- Hymns are sung at religious services;
- Dancers perform to music surrounding them;
- Happy birthday is sung by families and friends;
- And performances by orchestras, open air concerts, choirs, and operas inspire us all.

Music is fun. Can you even imagine your life without it?

"... I listened, motionless and still;
And, as I mounted up the hill,
The music in my heart I bore,
Long after it was heard no more."
–William Wordsworth "The Solitary Reaper"

THE BLESSINGS OF BEAUTY

A Sleeping Mystery

Beauty is a sleeping mystery; ***a sleeping mystery only until we acknowledge it***. Appearing to be dormant when we first give it our attention, beauty gives meaning to our experience shortly thereafter, ***because it makes us feel***.

"There is a light that shines beyond all things on earth, beyond us all, beyond the heavens, beyond the highest, the very highest heavens. This is the light that shines in your heart." –The Chandogya Upanishad

Immersed in the experience of beauty just for a moment has the power to change us from within. Witness a newborn baby, a fully bloomed rose, or a peaceful death, ***and say you are not moved***.

"Beauty is the gift of God." –Aristotle

Beauty generates feelings of goodness, love, harmony, and peace. And it does not have to be just a serene happening. It can be a physical healing such as a tumor disappearing or mental anxiety turning peaceful. In fact there are many different things of beauty to find in our world, depending on how we look at them. Sometimes the most ugly thing among us turns out to be the most beautiful of all. And sometimes it's the reverse.

"It's not what you look at that matters, it's what you see." –Henry David Thoreau

The puffy white clouds against the deep blue sky can quickly turn from a scene of beauty when dark and stormy clouds appear. A campfire glowing in the dark with brilliant flames of yellow, orange and red mesmerizes us until it turns wild and generates fear.

Beauty is a force unto itself that each person experiences in their own way. For some it is a force of influence while others see it as a quality or a perception. But no matter how we define it, the power of beauty is real. **The power of beauty is real *because in its presence we are changed*.**

"But there is nothing that makes its way more directly into the soul than beauty..." –Joseph Addison

Just imagine the beauty of the blessings in disguise in past heroes like Thomas Edison, Louis Pasteur, Madame Currie, Jackie Robinson, Rosa Parks, and many more who sought out the blessings from themselves that made the world a better place for so many others to enjoy.

"Beauty can inspire miracles." –Benjamin Disraeli

Beauty can be found by looking for the good in every person we meet. Even if we do not immediately find it, the beauty lies in our looking for it.

"Though we travel the world over to find the beautiful, we must carry it with us or we find it not."
–Ralph Waldo Emerson

The beauty of our spirit shines through when we allow ourselves to see new meaning from the things that hurt us the most. And when bad things happen to good people, there are many others who come forward to help. It is then we discover the great wisdom shared by ancient masters.

BLESSINGS FOUND IN DISGUISE

A river of peace, harmony, and joy

THE POWER OF BLESSINGS

The great Jewish Sage, Rabbi Abraham Joshua Heschel, said:

"Just to be is a blessing. Just to live is holy."

By learning the art of blessing we discover ourselves in a deeper way. For when we bless, we reach into our innermost being in a state of unconditional love to wish total good for another. When we bless, it strengthens our sense of gratitude, opens our heart, and we thus experience the world as *blessed* rather than threatening.

A wonderful way to start each day is to bless it.

"Every morning we are born again. What we do today is what matters most." –Gautama Buddha

We bless more than we realize sometimes in ordinary, simple ways that affect those around us.

- Returning a lost item;
- Giving a big hug when needed;
- Sharing an invitation to an event;
- Cooking a meal for a friend who is ill;

- A ride to the doctor or hospital;
- Devoting undivided attention to a meaningful conversation;
- Offering help by running an errand;
- A simple "how are you" call.

Blessings are not always packaged as we expect–some are well disguised and hidden. Some of our worst experiences are blessings that change our lives for the better.

"Every experience, no matter how bad it seems, holds within it a blessing of some kind. The goal is to find it."
–Gautama Buddha

Some daily blessings we often forget to be thankful for are:

- Being alive yet another day;
- Free will to make choices;
- Our body's natural healing ability;
- Our eyes to read, navigate, and see beauty;
- A flash of insight out of the blue;
- Our feet that carry us to and fro;
- Our pets welcoming us home;
- Having a roof over our head.

William Wordsworth in his poem "Lines Written A Few Miles above Tintern Abbey" put it so beautifully when he said:

"...all which we behold Is full of blessings..."

Kahlil Gibran, author of *The Prophet* ("On Pain") says:

"...And could you keep your heart in wonder at the daily miracles of your life, your pain would not seem less wondrous than your joy;..."

There is no limit to where daily blessings can take you. Slow down and catch the beautiful moments in front of you that are presented as blessings. Always be on the lookout for who or what you can bless today:

- The city in which you live;
- Passersby on the street;
- Patients in hospitals and nursing homes;
- Students and teachers in schools;
- Policemen, firemen, and first responders;
- *the list goes on and on....*

"...All things are bound together. All things connect."
– Chief Seattle, Duwamish and Suquamish

It has been said that every time we bless another, the blessing returns to us increased. Is there any wonder then why we should not learn to bless? ***This is the power of blessing***.

"How far that little candle throws its beams! So shines a good deed..." –William Shakespeare, "The Merchant of Venice"

BLESSED FRIENDSHIPS AND RELATIONSHIPS

Immeasurable!

Good friends give us a sense of belonging and acceptance. They listen to our worries without judgment, share our tears and laughter, give us a hug, and are there when we need them most.

Relationships can also give us a sense of belonging and acceptance. But relationships and friendships are different. We have relationships that will not always be friendships. However, good relationships always present us with the opportunity to create new friendships.

"At times our own light goes out and is rekindled by a spark from another person. Each of us has cause to think with deep gratitude of those who have lighted the flame within us." –Albert Schweitzer

We have relationships with our mother, our father, our sisters and brothers. We have relationships with our aunts, uncles, cousins, and animals too. We have relationships with a higher power and Mother Earth. We have relationships with ourselves and significant others.

Relationships are a give-and-take situation. They have a beginning and end, but should never be all or nothing. Some seek deeper spiritual connections while others seek only surface connections, but all can help us find a greater understanding of our role in life.

"We cannot live only for ourselves. A thousand fibers connect us with our fellow men;..."–Herman Melville

When we cultivate deep friendships in our relationships, we demonstrate not only kindness but also forgiveness and compassion. This helps us to heal divides and build a more compassionate world.

"And let there be no purpose in friendship save the deepening of the spirit." –Kahlil Gibran, The Prophet, *("On Friendship")*

Friendships are treasures that enrich our soul. One of life's greatest blessings, friends are a priceless gift to be cherished and celebrated. Having a true friend by your side is a reminder that we are never alone.

"A true friend is the greatest of all blessings, and that which we take the least care of all to acquire."
 –Francois de La Rochefoucauld

WE ARE HERE FOR EACH OTHER

Relationships and friendships provide valuable advice and guidance for us to ponder. The power of connection is strong. Others often see the best in us, inspire us, and believe in us even more than we believe in ourselves.

While connecting with others we can have fun, we can be kind, we can be loving, and most of all we can be friends.

"And in the sweetness of friendship let there be laughter, and sharing of pleasures. For in the dew of little things, the heart finds its morning and is refreshed." –Kahlil Gibran, The Prophet *("On Friendship)"*

Traditional Irish blessings convey hope, happiness, and good fortune for relationships and friendships. May their powerful messages fill your heart.

"May God grant you always...
A sunbeam to warm you,
A moonbeam to charm you,
A sheltering angel so nothing can harm you.
Laughter to cheer you,
Faithful friends near you.
And whenever you pray,
Heaven to hear you."

"May God give you ...
For every storm, a rainbow,
For every tear, a smile,
For every care, a promise,
And a blessing in each trial.
For every problem life sends,
A faithful friend to share,
For every sigh, a sweet song,
And an answer for each prayer."

"May the road rise up to meet you,
May the wind be always at your back,
May the sun shine warm upon your face,
The rains fall soft upon your fields,
And until we meet again,
May God hold you in the palm of His hand."

BLESSINGS OF OLD

Unique and powerful, many Native American blessings influence our lives with peace, love, and gratitude.

In the language of their times, these ancient authors continue to intrigue us. What blessings did they want to convey that still hold meaning for us today? Did they understand the concept of prayer that we still seek? Is it possible they were trying to tell us that changing our course of action, even in a very small way, might reflect our entire future?

We may never uncover the answers to these questions but for the beautiful writings they left behind.

"...There is one God looking down on us all. We are all the children of one God. The sun, the darkness, the winds are all listening to what we have to say."
     –Geronimo 1829-1909 Apache

How we relate to the world and one another might be more important than we fully realize. Truly these ancient authors wanted to influence future generations when leaving their valuable messages carved in stone.

"The first peace, which is the most important, is that which comes within the souls of people when they realize their relationship, their oneness with the universe and all its powers, and when they realize at the center of the universe dwells the Great Spirit, and that its center is really everywhere, it is within each of us." –Black Elk 1863-1950, Oglala Lakota

Native American cultures are rich in spiritual and religious traditions. From offering prayers to the Great Spirit to honoring beauty and nature, their blessings provide a way to honor and celebrate the sacredness of life.

"...Earth teach me freedom
*   as the eagle which soars in the sky.*
Earth teach me resignation
*   as the leaves which die in the fall.*
Earth teach me regeneration
*   as the seed which rises in the spring.*
Earth teach me to forget myself
*   as melted snow forgets its life.*
Earth teach me to remember kindness
*   as dry fields weep with rain."*
–Ute Prayer

"To be able to greet the sun with the sounds from all of Nature is a great blessing, and it helps us to remember Who is the real provider of all our benefits." –Thomas Yellowtail 1903-1993 Crow

"...Grandfather,
Sacred One,
Teach us love, compassion and honor
That we may heal the earth
And heal each other." –Ojibway Prayer

"May the stars carry your sadness away,
May the flowers fill your heart with beauty,
May hope forever wipe away your tears,
And, above all, may silence make you strong."
–Chief Dan George 1899-1981 Tsleil-Waututh

A WORD ABOUT GOD

"In the beginning was the Word, and the Word was with God, and the Word was God. The same was in the beginning with God. All things were made by him; without him was not any thing made that was made."
–John 1:1-3 King James Bible

Though God is a mystery, He makes Himself known to those who seek Him. Those with open minds and hearts gain a lot through open-minded discussion and listening. God does not overstep *the free will* given to every person having a human experience.

SPIRITUAL BLESSINGS

Take a venture into the Bible, and you will find countless blessings, stories, and verses of practical use. Messages provided eons ago still ring true. Some are structured to keep us on the straight and narrow, and others lay a path of mercy, compassion, and forgiveness.

Here are some verses from the Bible to ponder:

"It is more blessed to give than to receive." (Acts 20:35)

*"The LORD bless you and keep you;
the LORD make his face shine on you
    and be gracious to you;
the LORD turn his face toward you and give you
    peace." –Numbers 6:24-26*

THE BEATITUDES

There are eight beatitudes, a set of teachings Jesus gave us in the Sermon on the Mount in the Gospel of Matthew. (5:1-12) The purpose is to inspire us to live according to the traits Jesus described and to show the rewards we will receive.

"Blessed are the poor in spirit, for theirs is the kingdom of heaven."

"Blessed are those who mourn, for they shall be comforted."

"Blessed are the meek, for they shall inherit the earth."

"Blessed are they who hunger and thirst for righteousness, for they shall be filled."

"Blessed are the merciful, for they shall obtain mercy."

"Blessed are the pure of heart, for they shall see God."

"Blessed are the peacemakers, for they shall be called children of God."

"Blessed are they who are persecuted for righteousness' sake, for theirs is the kingdom of heaven."

ONLY GOD

"Only God is limitless;
Only God can sustain a prairie;
Only God can create a flower with no beginning;
Only God can raise a mountain out of the sea;
Only God creates marvelous creatures
     in the deep dark ocean;
The gift of life is the truth of God, you and me.
God is limitless, boundless and all-knowing.
We are limited. Only God is limitless."
– Katherine Scherer

EPILOGUE

Life is a Privilege, a Precious Journey, a Blessing

Life is a precious gift from God. We recognize it as a blessing when we focus on what we have instead of what we lack. Not only are we blessed, but we have the power to bless and to be a blessing to others just by wishing and wanting the best for them. When we bless others, we become a vessel of grace bringing joy into the lives of those around us. By living with an open heart ready to give and receive blessings, we create a cycle of love, a powerful energy that extends far beyond ourselves.

"...What is life? It is the flash of a firefly in the night. It is the breath of a buffalo in the wintertime. It is the little shadow which runs across the grass and tosses itself in the sunset." –Chief Crowfoot, 1830- 1890
Blackfoot Indian Chief

The Butterfly Effect

Have you ever heard of the butterfly effect? The butterfly effect can be somewhat humbling by helping us realize that there is much more to the makings of this world than one could ever perceive.

It has been said that a butterfly flapping its wings in Brazil could eventually cause a tornado in Texas. Though it sounds incredible like a fable, **it can actually happen**. Imagine for a moment the power in that one subtle movement of a butterfly's wings.

Imagine for a moment, the power in your own words when blessing another.

"We cannot hold a torch to light another's path without brightening our own." –Ben Sweetland

Adversity Can Be a Blessing

It is true that there are many, many more blessings that we are endowed with than those mentioned in this work. Even our adversities can have a positive effect if we choose to learn from them. Adversity and challenge prepare us for difficulty. That is why when bad things happen to good people, they can be said to be a blessing. Let us pray that if adversity comes to us, we are prepared for it.

It's important to understand that blessings are not just material possessions or tangible things. Blessings can take on a spiritual dimension such as a sense of purpose, inner peace and a meaningful relationship with a higher power. Some blessings are obvious like a promotion at work or the birth of a child; other blessings are quiet and subtle, like the feeling of contentment at the beauty in nature. Being blessed can mean having good luck or fortune, experiencing a sense of well-being, or simply recognizing and appreciating the positive aspects of our lives. Blessings are often viewed as divine favor, grace, and kindness from God.

Gratitude Works

Practicing gratitude is one of the key ways to truly recognize blessings. It is a powerful force that can help shift our perspective towards the positive. When we make a conscious effort to focus on what we have and be thankful for it, we can open up a whole new world of abundance. Gratitude increases happiness and positivity, reduces stress and anxiety, and boosts self-esteem and confidence.

"Wear gratitude like a cloak and it will feed every corner of your life." –Rumi

Being grateful for simple things like a sunset or a kind word can turn innocent moments into joy and appreciation. Blessings are not always big dramatic events. Often they're small moments of grace; gifts that come quietly but have a lasting impact. When we recognize these moments, we begin to see that life itself is a blessing filled with countless opportunities to give and receive.

There is no blessing more appropriate than the one that we wish for you here:

"May your days be many and your troubles be few.
May all God's blessings descend upon you.
May peace be within you.
May your heart be strong.
May you find what you're seeking wherever you roam." –Irish Blessing

ABOUT THE AUTHORS

Katherine Scherer and Eileen Bodoh who reside in Milwaukee, Wisconsin, are authors of *Gratitude Works: Open Your Heart to Love* and contributing authors in *101 Ways to Improve Your Health* published by www.selfgrowth.com. As guest authors in publications, newsletters and radio broadcasts, their articles were featured in Florida, California, New Mexico, Wisconsin, Michigan, Minnesota, and Canada.

www.ingramcontent.com/pod-product-compliance
Lightning Source LLC
Chambersburg PA
CBHW061255040426
42444CB00010B/2393